THE
ABCs
OF A TREASURED LIFE

Chase,
Never give up
in your quest to
live a treasured
life. The word
of God lights the way
to a treasured life.

James H Sullivan

THE ABCs OF A TREASURED LIFE

© 2018 by James H. Sullivan

Design and layout: Carolyn B. Smith

Scripture quotations marked HCSB are taken from the HOLMAN CHRISTIAN STANDARD BIBLE, copyright 1999, 2000, 2002, 2003 by Holman Bible Publishers, Nashville, Tennessee. All rights reserved.

Scripture quotations marked KJV are taken from the Holy Bible, KING JAMES VERSION; public domain.

Scripture quotations marked NCV are taken from the Holy Bible, NEW CENTURY VERSION, copyright 2005 by Thomas Nelson, Inc. Used by permission. All rights reserved.

Scripture quotations marked NIV are taken from the HOLY BIBLE, NEW INTERNATIONAL VERSION. Copyright 1973, 1978, 1984, 2011 by Biblica, Inc. Used by permission of Zondervan. All rights reserved.

Scripture quotations marked NLT are taken from the HOLY BIBLE, NEW LIVING TRANSLATION. Copyright 1996, 2004, 2007 by Tyndale House Foundation. Used by permission of Tyndale House Publishers, Inc., Carol Stream, Illinois 60188. All rights reserved.

ISBN: 978-1727090079

TABLE OF CONTENTS

ENDORSEMENTS

From his years of experience as an educator, "cultural listener,"
and pastor, James writes with a gentle passion. A passion to see lives
preserved and transformed to their best. Using a simple A, B, C
approach, this book is a gift to all who read it.
—*Dr. Daryl L. Smith*, Emeritus Professor of Mentoring and Leadership,
Asbury Seminary—Florida

This is a book you'll truly treasure and read again and again.
It's perfect for using in your daily devotional time or any time you need a
refreshing word from the Lord to apply along this journey we call "life."
—*Bria Sullivan*, Certified Life Coach and Founder, b. sulli coaching

Early in life as a child, we learned our ABCs. How prolific that
James Sullivan takes the ABCs to create a book on living a treasured life
aimed at youth. *The ABCs of a Treasured Life* is an uplifting collection of
thoughts based on scriptural reference and activities for reflection as well
as steps for taking action. The ideas are lyrical and cover varied, relevant
topics designed to teach and inspire its readers to treasure the life that
God has given them. This makes for an engaging read that, although
aimed at youth, is applicable for everyone.
—*Kevin G. Perry*, Ph. D., St. Lucie Public Schools

Each day is a gift from God! As they say when flying on airplanes, "Put the oxygen mask on yourself before you try to help others." *The ABCs of a Treasured Life* is an outstanding, practical book on how to get in touch with your personal values before forming relationships to help others. We can all relate very easily to our ABCs and how we used them to start with the basics of learning. At the end of each lettered chapter are practical activities related to Scriptures and quotes that provide excellent gems of thought in developing a treasured life.
—*Dr. Cleve Henry*, Educational Consultant, Retired Adjunct Professor

The ABCs of a Treasured Life is a spiritually uplifting book. It is very valuable for expanding and enhancing the biblical knowledge of youth as well as adults. It is easy to read and practical. James Sullivan uses the letters of the alphabet as an effective aid to help readers memorize the values discussed in this book. Thanks for being an inspiration to our family!
—*Janice Williams*, Youth Director, Mt. Pleasant Primitive Baptist Church

James Sullivan's *The ABCs of a Treasured Life* is an excellent guide for anyone interested in experiencing a wonderful Christian journey through life. His use of the alphabet is a simple approach to illustrating how to use this book as a guide while incorporating God in our daily lives. It is a great motivational tool for family and friends who seek to strengthen their relationship with God as well as each other. I highly recommend this book as a part of your daily reading.
—*Representative Larry Lee, Jr.,* Florida House of Representatives, District 84

ACKNOWLEDGEMENTS

The ABCs of a Treasured Life is a reflection of the guiding principles and values that have shaped my life and continue to be my moral and spiritual compass in living the life that God has called me to live. There are many people to thank for encouraging me to write this book, and for contributing to its completion. Foremost, I thank my Lord and Savior for the vision, the opportunity and the inspiration.

I have been truly blessed with family, friends, colleagues, and mentors beyond those listed here who have positively impacted my life. Some of them have endorsed this book, or they have been mentioned elsewhere. To those not mentioned, I am sure you know who you are, and I say a heartfelt *thank you!*

For my parents (both deceased), **Henry and Clara Mae Sullivan**—I give thanks for rearing me and my four siblings (**Fred, Henri Mae, Willie, and Elma**) in a Christian home where the qualities and values discussed in this book were not only taught, but modeled, and lived.

Bertha—my life partner for more than 48 years, I thank you for your belief in me, your love, prayers, commitment, and devotion as we have endeavored each day to live a treasured life together.

Our son, **James, Jr,** (and wife **Natalie**), and daughter, **Bria**—you have helped us to expand the meaning and experience of living a treasured life by sharing it with you and learning as well from you.

Thank you to **Christian Henry**, our wonderful grandson. You have captured our hearts and given us moments to treasure beyond anything we could have imagined. We pray that, just as we have (and your parents have), you will learn from the life examples before you what it means to live a treasured life.

I am also indebted to and grateful the following persons for their contributions to this book:

Dr. Daryl L. Smith, Emeritus Professor of Mentoring and Leadership, Asbury Seminary—Florida. No words can adequately convey my sincere thanks for the opportunity to learn from you, to contribute in some small way to your Small Group Ministry publications, as well as for the encouragement and valuable help you have given me in my first solo publication. To you, I will always be grateful.

Lillie M. Fenderson, lifetime family friend, and retired Professor of English, Seminole Community College—Orlando, Florida. Thank you for the careful and meticulous edits of this book not only once, but several times! Your reviews have been indispensable to helping me to communicate effectively what I wanted to say.

Carolyn B. Smith, Communications Director, United Methodist Church. I am indebted to you for your tireless, creative efforts in typesetting and formatting this book with graphics and a cover design that contribute to easy reading and artistic appeal.

INTRODUCTION

The gift of life is no ordinary present. It is not like the gifts people give during birthdays, weddings, anniversaries, at Christmas or any other special times of the year. It is much more than that. Life is an extraordinary gift given to all humankind by the Living and True God in whose image we are created. It is to be treasured more than glittering gold or precious rubies, fine diamonds, or expensive china. We are the crowning gift of all creation. As such, our lives should be lived in a manner that brings glory to our creator and adds beauty to all creation.

The idea for this book was conceived during a time when senseless violence gripped our small community and the lives of several youths who were just beginning to live were snuffed out as though they never mattered. Our stunned community and city were in disbelief, denial, and dismay that anyone for whatever reason would have such a lack of appreciation and respect for a life they did not create and could not sustain or redeem. Yet, three seemingly innocent lives were taken with complete disregard for the simple axiom, "Live and let live." This is a problem that still persists today, not just in our community, but everywhere in our world. Unfortunately, since the inception of this book things have gotten, and continue to get, worse rather than better.

In my role as a clergy liaison with Treasure Coast Hospice, I, along with Sonya' Finney, a diversity consultant with TCH, and Catherine Huynh, community outreach coordinator, had been given the task of engaging youth from local churches in a project that would teach them something about the importance of treasuring life. The tragic shootings in our community were a catalyst for a play that several young people from local churches wrote under the direction of Nicole Stoddard. This play, "The Choice of Life," was performed for the entire community. When the performances were over, the young people who participated in this effort asked us, "Where do we go from here?" and "What do we do now?" Several ideas were pursued but none were ever developed.

The ABCs of a Treasured Life is written in response to the question asked by the wonderful young people who gave up many Saturdays to participate in engaging activities designed to help them to appreciate their own lives so that they could both apply it and then share it with others. I hope every reader will find something to treasure from reading and engaging in the activities included in each chapter in this book. I dedicate it to anyone who wants to live a life that makes a difference and who seeks to honor God our Creator through life-changing moments of inspiration, meditation, and reflection.

"Today I have given you a choice between life and death, between blessings and curses. Now I call on heaven and earth to witness the choice you make. Oh, that you would choose life, so that you and your descendants might live! You can make this choice by loving the Lord your God, obeying him, and committing yourself firmly to him. This is the key to your life. And if you love and obey the Lord, you will live long in the land the Lord swore to give your ancestors, Abraham, Isaac, and Jacob."
—Deuteronomy 30:19–20 (NLT)

"The word of God lights the path to a treasured life."

HOW TO USE THIS BOOK

This book was written mainly with an audience of youth and young adults in mind. It can be a good resource with many practical uses depending upon the intent of the reader. With its emphasis on Scripture, it can be used by those committed to following Christ. The following list is offered as some suggestions:

- It can be used by young people seeking to find meaning and value in life as they prepare to face the world as adults.
- Young people, as well as adults, can use this book as a daily devotional for scriptural guidance, spiritual growth, personal development, and personal reflection.
- It can be used as a study and discussion guide for accountability groups, and small group ministry.
- Parents can use portions of *The ABCs of a Treasured Life* to teach their children about important values for success in life.
- It can be used with youth groups as a guide for teaching character building and values clarification.
- It can be used as a motivational guide inspiring readers to live a treasured life.
- It can be used as a how-to guide for showing respect for all human life.
- It can be used as an inspirational guide to developing a positive self-concept.
- The **In Search of a Treasured Life**, **Related Scriptures**, and **Coins for your Treasure Chest** sections at the end of each chapter are provided to engage readers in further study for personal and spiritual growth in the specific attributes discussed.

ACCEPTANCE AND APPRECIATION

*"Accept, our Father, the offering of our faith
and our words and our lives."*
—Howard Thurman, *The Centering Moment*

YOUR LIFE IS TO BE TREASURED. SHOW **ACCEPTANCE** *AND*
APPRECIATION *OF YOUR LIFE AS A PRECIOUS GIFT FROM* GOD.

 KEY SCRIPTURE

*For you created my inmost being, you knit me together in my mother's womb.
I will praise you because I am fearfully and wonderfully made; your works are
wonderful, I know that full well.* —Psalm 139:13–14 (NIV)

In verses 13–14 of Psalm 139, David seems to be in awe and wonder of the
God who gave him life and of the life that God had given him. He praises God
because God is all-knowing, ever-present, and all-powerful. As he did with
David, God certainly knew what he was doing when he made you and me.

Acceptance is the act of receiving something offered or given by someone
else. **Appreciation** is being grateful or thankful for something that has
been given to you. True appreciation comes from heartfelt recognition of
the gift and the giver. The gift is life, a life to be valued, a life to be trea-

sured, a life to be lived to the fullest. The giver is God, the true and living God. God is not only the source of the precious gift of life, but He is also the one who provides for us, sustains us, and redeems us. To accept your life as a gift from God is an act of both humility and honor.

Psalm 100 invites us to *"know that the Lord is God. It is he who made us, and we are his; we are his people, and the sheep of his pasture"* (Psalm 100:3, NIV).

My acceptance and appreciation of the life given to me moves me to give thanks with joy and vitality. With gratefulness, humility, and thankfulness I accept and appreciate the life that God has given me. I am comfortable with the fact that God knows the plans He has for me (Jeremiah 29:11), and I completely trust him with my life.

My Acceptance Speech

Dear Lord, I graciously and gratefully accept and appreciate my life as a precious gift from you. It is too wonderful for me to comprehend that you knew me before I was conceived in my mother's womb. But this is true of you, the living God who exists in the "eternal now." Even before time began, you are God. You are actively existent in my past, my present, and my future. When I look back over my life, I clearly see your hand guiding me, your arms carrying me, your grace blessing me, and your mercy forgiving me. In my "now", you show yourself the same as in my yesterday. I cannot imagine tomorrow without you.

Father, I want to use my life to your glory and to your honor. I want to live it, use it and not abuse it. I want to relish and cherish it as a syrupy sweet. I want to make my life count by living with conviction, direction, devotion and purpose. Heavenly Father, I give my life back to you in the melody of this moment, the rhythms of this day, and the symphony of the years as a reflection of you in whose image I was created. Thank you for my life, Lord. I realize that all the gifts of life and healing come from your initiative. I give my consent in this acceptance speech for you to use my life as you will. Here I am Lord, send me. Amen.

🔍 IN SEARCH OF A TREASURED LIFE

Perhaps you are not at a point in your life where you are willing to accept and appreciate the life God has given you. Write three things you believe need to happen before you can accept and appreciate your life. Write the name of someone who can help you on your quest:

Before I can appreciate my life, I need to	I can ask for help from:
1.	1.
2.	2.
3.	3.

In order to keep focused when completing a task, it is good to set a time-frame to get things done. Write a reasonable timeframe in which you would expect to get this done.

I expect to get help with my needs from the persons identified above by _____ so I can write my **Acceptance Speech** to God by _____.

"I can only be right with God if I accept the atonement of Jesus Christ as an absolute gift."—Oswald Chambers

Think about God's gift of life to you personally based upon where you are in your relationship with Christ right now. Write your own Acceptance Speech to God. Use the author's acceptance speech as an example. Length does not matter. What matters is that it comes from your heart.

My Acceptance Speech

_____

_____

_____

_____

_____

_____

_____. Amen

RELATED SCRIPTURES ABOUT ACCEPTANCE AND APPRECIATION

(If you want to read more about what the Bible says about **acceptance** and **appreciation**, here are some related Scriptures. You may find others in your Bible reading. If you do, add them to the list.)

Genesis 1:27
Job 10:12
Ecclesiastes 5:19–20
Ecclesiastes 12:1–7
Isaiah 42:5–6
Acts 17:24–25

COINS FOR YOUR TREASURE CHEST

(This section contains additional quotes from other sources or thoughts written by the author. If you find more quotes on this topic, please add them along with the source of the quote.)

We cannot respect God's gift of life to others until we treasure the life God has given to us.

BALANCE

"The healthy expansion of the spiritual life
depends on the balance struck between two movements;
the direction of the soul's love and energy first towards God,
and then towards other men."
—Evelyn Underhill, *Concerning the Inner Life*

---

*Y*OUR LIFE IS TO BE TREASURED. **BALANCE** YOUR LIFE AS *J*ESUS DID
BY LIVING AND ACTING IN A MANNER THAT IS PLEASING TO *G*OD.

 KEY SCRIPTURE

Jesus became wiser and grew physically. People liked him,
and he pleased God.—Luke 2:52 (NCV)

Balance is the state of stability and harmony. To have balance in your life is to live with your emotions, behavior, moral, social, mental, intellectual, physical, and spiritual development on an equal footing. To have balance is to be well-rounded and grounded in the word of God. One who finds balance in life pleases God and gains favor with people.

The best example I can give of the kind of balance that characterizes a treasured life is the description of Jesus found in Luke 2:52. Jesus' growth and development was described as increasing in wisdom *(intellectual)*; stature *(physical)*; in favor with God *(spiritual)*; and in favor with people *(social)*. This kind of balance ultimately affects our behavior (the way we conduct ourselves). To treasure our lives implies in the most complete sense that our goal is to please God, our Creator. Behaving in a manner that finds favor with God, for one who is already a Christian, will generally lead to having genuine favor with humankind.

$\mathcal{Q}$ IN SEARCH OF A TREASURED LIFE

On a scale of 1–5, with five being the highest, rate yourself as to where you feel that you are at this point in your life in achieving **balance** in the following areas:

1. Emotional ____
2. Behavior ____
3. Moral ____
4. Social ____
5. Mental ____
6. Intellectual ____
7. Physical ____
8. Spiritual ____

What are your lowest areas? Why do you think these areas are low for you?

Develop one strategy for improving in three of the low areas you have identified and find a significant person in your life to help with your development and hold you accountable. Using the lines on the next page, list the area where you need to improve, the person(s) who will help with your development in the area identified, and the timeframe for completion of this strategy. Your timeframe can be expressed in weeks, months or by a specific date. At the end of the specified time, discuss your progress with the person(s) who have helped you. Make adjustments as needed.

Area needing improvement	Who will hold me accountable?	Timeframe to improve

"Do not waver, for a person with divided loyalty is as unsettled as a wave of the sea that is blown and tossed by the wind. Such people should not expect to receive anything from the Lord. Their loyalty is divided between God and the world, and they are unstable in everything they do."—James 1:6–8 (NLT)

James 1:8 speaks about the balance between the heart and the mind. How can having an unhealthy balance between your heart and your mind threaten your physical, mental, emotional, and spiritual well-being?

Choose one:

_____ (a) I could make foolish, costly mistakes.

_____ (b) People may not know how to take me.

_____ (c) I could come across as an airhead.

_____ (d) My relationships could suffer.

_____ (e) other _____

Write down one thing that you can do right now to achieve more balance in your life:

_____.

RELATED SCRIPTURES ABOUT BALANCE

(If you want to read more about what the Bible says about **balance**, here are some related Scriptures. You may find others in your Bible reading. If you do, add them to the list.)

Proverbs 11:1; 16:11; 20:23
Isaiah 40:12, 15

COINS FOR YOUR TREASURE CHEST

(Ideas in this section are additional quotes from other sources or thoughts written by the author. If you find more quotes on this topic, please add them along with the source of the quote.)

"Life is a balance of holding on and letting go."
—Rumi

CONTENTMENT

"A contented mind is the greatest blessing a man can enjoy in this world: and if in the present life his happiness arises from the subduing of his desires, it will arise in the next from the gratification of them."
—Joseph Addison

---

*Y*OUR LIFE IS TO BE TREASURED. *L*EARN TO HAVE **CONTENTMENT** IN WHATEVER CIRCUMSTANCE YOU FIND YOURSELF.

 KEY SCRIPTURE

For I have learned in whatsoever state I am, therewith to be content.
—Philippians 4:11 (KJV)

Contentment is the state of being satisfied. Sometimes in life we find ourselves in stressful situations and in places where we don't want or need to be. It is important during these times for us to remember what the Apostle Paul says in Philippians 4:11–13. Paul learned through the "ups" and "downs" in his own life that God is always in control. Contentment does not depend on the circumstances in our life. Contentment is the evidence of complete trust in the God who loves us.

The Apostle Paul said to believers in the church at Philippi, *"I can do all things through Christ who gives me strength"* (Philippians 4:13, KJV). This should also give us the assurance that through Christ we can adapt to any situation or circumstance we may encounter in our lives. Contentment is doing our best with what we have, wherever we are because we believe that God is with us. Contentment is being happy with the necessities of life and not worrying about the luxuries. Contentment is living within our means and not coveting what somebody else has been given. It is not just tolerating living; it is celebrating being alive. Are you satisfied with your life?

IN SEARCH OF A TREASURED LIFE

"God has a special place in his heart for me and a special purpose for me to fulfill in this world."
—Carl Dreizler and Mary E. Ehemann, from "52 Ways to Lose Weight"

Remind yourself to be contented by repeating the quotation above three times a day for the next 30 days.

"Don't worry about anything; instead, pray about everything. Tell God what you need, and thank him for all he has done. Then you will experience God's peace, which exceeds anything we can understand. His peace will guard your hearts and minds as you live in Christ Jesus."
—Philippians 4:6–7 (NLT)

After reading Philippians 4:6–7, make a list of three requests you need to bring before God in prayer. Pray that God will give you contentment with your present situation and faith to trust that God will supply your needs when the time is right:

1. _____

2. _____

3. _____

RELATED SCRIPTURES ABOUT CONTENTMENT

(If you want to read more about what the Bible says about **contentment**, here are some related Scriptures. You may find others in your Bible reading. If you do, add them to the list.)

Psalms 23:1-3
Proverbs 14:30; 15:15; 17:22; 23:17–18; 51:10, 12
Isaiah 26:3
John 14:27
1 Corinthians 4:14–18
Philippians 4:6-7
Hebrews 13:5
1Timothy 6:6–7
1 Peter 1:3; 5:7

COINS FOR YOUR TREASURE CHEST

(Entries in this section are additional quotes from other sources or thoughts written by the author. If you find more quotes on this topic, please add them along with the source of the quote.)

Contentment is the assurance of knowing that God is with you whether you are in the pit or the palace.
—Carl Dreizler and Mary Ehemann

DISCIPLINE

"Good Character is that quality which makes one dependable, whether being watched or not, which makes one truthful when it is to one's advantage to be a little less that truthful, which makes one courageous when faced with great obstacles, which endows one with firmness of wise self-discipline."
—Arthur S. Adams

YOUR LIFE IS TO BE TREASURED.
DO YOUR BEST TO LIVE A **DISCIPLINED** *LIFE .*

 ## KEY SCRIPTURE

When I learn your righteous laws, I will thank you by living as I should!
—Psalm 119:7 (NLT)

Discipline means having self-control. Self-discipline is the ability to go after your goals in an orderly way. Without order, there is chaos. When there is chaos in our lives, the chances of failure at what we try to do are maximized. More than "talking the talk," self-discipline is "walking the walk" each day, whether we are being noticed or not; whether we want to or not. Without discipline, our lives have little meaning, and we aimlessly live our lives without direction or focus. There is no clear path to take, and any thing we choose seems right. When we treasure our lives, we seek to be disciplined physically, morally, mentally, and spiritually. We obey the word of God and follow the example of Christ.

🔍 IN SEARCH OF A TREASURED LIFE

How disciplined are you at this time in your life? Check one:
- (   ) very
- (   ) as disciplined as I should be
- (   ) somewhat
- (   ) I'm not sure
- (   ) not at all.

Identify an area in your life where you need to become more self-disciplined and write it down here:

_____

Describe what your life might look like if you were disciplined in this area.

_____

What are **three steps** you can take now to become more disciplined in this area?
1. _____,
2. _____, and
3. _____.

Develop a **timeline** for implementing these strategies and note the date and time when you feel you have improved in the area you identified.

To become more disciplined in the area of _____, I will:
1. _____ by _____.
2. _____ by _____.
3. _____ by _____.

Completion Date: _____

Read these words from Psalm 1. After giving them some thought, write in the spaces that follow, two or three sentences that tell how these two verses have helped, or can help you live a more disciplined life:

"Oh, the joys of those who do not follow the advice of the wicked, or stand around with sinners, or join in with mockers, but they delight in the law of the Lord, meditating on it day and night."
—Psalm 1:1–2 (NLT)

_____

_____

_____

_____

_____

_____

RELATED SCRIPTURES ABOUT DISCIPLINE

(If you want to read more about what the Bible says about **discipline**, here are some related Scriptures. You may find others in your Bible reading. If you do, add them to the list.)

Psalm 1; 119:35
Romans 12:1–2
2 Corinthians 10:5
2 Peter 1:5-8
Jude 1:2–21

COINS FOR YOUR TREASURE CHEST

(Entries in this section are additional quotes from other sources or thoughts written by the author. If you find more quotes on this topic, please add them along with the source of the quote.)

"If we allow ourselves to live the undisciplined life of a careless disciple, casually allowing negative thoughts entrance, residence, and nourishment in our minds, then we are our own worst enemy."
—Robert H. Schuller

ENDURANCE

*"The heights by great men reached and kept were not attained
by sudden flight, but they while their companions slept,
were toiling upward in the night."*
—Henry Wadsworth Longfellow

YOUR LIFE IS TO BE TREASURED. DEVELOP THE HABIT OF
ENDURANCE *BY NEVER GIVING UP.*

 **KEY SCRIPTURE**

But the one who stands firm to the end will be saved.
—Matthew 24:13 (NLT)

Endurance is the ability to withstand or to continue. It is what enables one to persevere sometimes against what seem to be insurmountable odds. A person who values life will learn to persistently work toward accomplishing self-identified goals rather than becoming paralyzed by the difficulties of the moment.

The key to developing endurance is this: we cannot do it through our own strength. We need God. Remember, it is God who gave us life and this same God is always present in our lives. Jesus promises in Matthew 24:13 that those who will endure to the very end will be saved to live with him one day. The sweetness of the victory always follows the sweat of the work.

🔍 IN SEARCH OF A TREASURED LIFE

Review your search from the previous chapter on Discipline. What area did you identify where you need to become more self-disciplined? Are you persistently working to achieve the goal you set? If not, what hinders you from persevering toward your goal? Are you trying to do this alone or are you asking God's help? Remember this thought: *"He conquers who endures"* (Perseus).

Think of something unpleasant or undesirable in your life that you over-came by not giving up. Write a few sentences describing how it made you feel and how you overcame it.

_____

_____

_____

_____

_____

_____

_____.

RELATED SCRIPTURES ABOUT ENDURANCE

(If you want to read more about what the Bible says about **endurance**, here are some related Scriptures. You may find others in your Bible reading. If you do, add them to the list.)

John 6:27
Romans 2:7
1 Corinthians 13:7
Galatians 6:9
2 Timothy 2:3, 10–12
Hebrews 10:36; 11:27; 12:1–3
James 1:12; 5:11
1 Peter 1:25; 4:13

COINS FOR YOUR TREASURE CHEST

(Entries in this section are additional quotes from other sources or thoughts written by the author. If you find more quotes on this topic, please add them along with the source of the quote.)

"Life isn't about waiting for the storm to pass; it's about learning to dance in the rain."—Vivian Greene

FAITH, FAMILY & FRIENDS

"All that I have seen teaches me to trust the creator for all that I haven't seen."
—Ralph Waldo Emerson

"The quality of your life is determined by the quality of the people in your life."
—H. Jackson Brown, Jr., *A Hero in Every Heart*

---

*YOUR LIFE IS TO BE TREASURED. MAKE YOUR **FAITH,** YOUR **FAMILY**
AND YOUR **FRIENDS** THE FOUNDATION FOR LIVING A GODLY LIFE.*

 KEY SCRIPTURES

This Good News tells us how God makes us right in his sight. This is accomplished from start to finish by faith. As the Scriptures say, it is through faith that a righteous person has life.—Romans 1:17 (NLT)

Children, obey your parents because you belong to the Lord, for this is the right thing to do. Honor your father and mother. This is the first of the Ten Commandments that ends with a promise. And this is the promise: If you honor your father and mother, you will live a long life, full of blessing.
—Ephesians 6:1–3 (NLT)

A friend loves at all times…—Proverbs 17:17a (NIV)

In Hebrews 11:1, we read that *"Faith is being sure of what we hope for and certain of what we do not see"* (NIV). **Faith** for the Christian believer is complete trust and confidence in God. That being said, one who has faith will obey the word of God. Faith in God motivates us to persevere through challenges and difficulties we most certainly will face in life. Don't expect faith to make things easy. Expect faith to make things possible.

Family support is very important for successfully living a godly life. The Apostle Paul in Ephesians 6 emphasizes the point that Christian parents will impart Christian values in the home that will carry over into all aspects of their children's lives. The challenge for parents is to be sure that spiritual discipline, along with unconditional love, undergirds parental authority. For those who, for various reasons, lack family support, the support of one's Christian family, as well as other parental figures, is very important. The whole family benefits when family members love and support one another. Children need to learn that it is good for them and others to live by rules.

A **friend** is someone you know well and of whom you are fond. A friend is kind, supportive, dependable, and honest with you. Sometimes criticism from a friend can initially hurt one deeply, but over time, because it is given out of love, criticism does not ruin the relationship. On the contrary, when constructive criticism from a friend is accepted, it is profitable in helping one to grow (see Proverbs 27:6).

A treasured life will be anchored by our faith, our family, and our friends.

To Be A Good Friend

1. Smile often.

2. Notice what you really enjoy and look for others who enjoy the same things.

3. Identify someone who has a need you can supply and offer your assistance.

4. Learn to like being alone with yourself. Note things about living that enrich your life and make them a part of your daily routines. If you are happy being with you, chances are others will like your company too.

5. Forget what you give, and remember what you receive.

6. Be the one who's doing while others are asking, "Is there anything I can do"?

7. Listen—even in silence.

—Adapted from Gloria Gaither, Sue Buchanan, Peggy Benson, and Joy Mackenzie, *Friends through Thick and Thin*

IN SEARCH OF A TREASURED LIFE

"Friendship improves happiness and abates misery, by doubling our joy, and dividing our grief."—Joseph Addison

After reading the above quote, think of a time when you were helped through a difficult situation because of the friendship of another. Briefly comment on how their help made you feel.

_____

_____

_____

_____

_____

RELATED SCRIPTURES ABOUT FAITH, FAMILY & FRIENDS

(If you want to read more about what the Bible says about **faith, family and friends**, here are some related Scriptures. You may find others in your Bible reading. If you do, add them to the list.)

Faith
Matthew 21:21
Hebrews 11:6; 12:1, 2
Ephesians 2:8; 3:17–19
1 Corinthians 16:13
2 Corinthians 5:7
Romans 1:17

Family
Genesis 12:3; 28:4
Leviticus 25:10
Jeremiah 31:1
Mark 3:31–35

Friends
Proverbs 18:24; 27:6, 10, 17
John 15:12–15
Psalm 119:63

COINS FOR YOUR TREASURE CHEST

(Entries in this section are additional quotes from other sources or thoughts written by the author. If you find more quotes on this topic, please add them along with the source of the quote.)

Faith

"So faith comes from hearing, that is, hearing the Good News about Christ."
—Romans 10:17 (NLT)

Family

"Family is a circle of acceptance, strength, faith, hope, and love."

Friends

"The joy of true friendship is the freedom to be one's self."

GLORIFY GOD

"I will praise you, O Lord my God, with all my heart;
I will glorify your name forever."
— Psalm 86:12 (NIV)

YOUR LIFE IS TO BE TREASURED. **GLORIFY GOD** *WHO LOVES YOU*
AND IS THE GIVER OF LIFE.

 KEY SCRIPTURE

For ye are bought with a price: therefore glorify God in your body,
and in your spirit, which are God's.
—1 Corinthians 6:20 (KJV)

To **glorify God** is to worship and praise God, the Source of all our blessings. When we glorify God, our lives reflect the image of God. God created the world and all things in it. God is the One who gives life and breath to us, and God alone is the One who satisfies our needs (Acts 17:24).

The Apostle Paul in 1 Corinthians 6:13–20 emphasized the fact that because

God gave us life, we belong to God. The Spirit of the Living God dwells within the heart of every believer because of the Holy Spirit. We treasure our lives when we freely accept salvation purchased by our Lord and Savior Jesus Christ through His death on the cross and resurrection to life everlasting. We should praise God for the unspeakable gift of His Son, Jesus, who came that we might have life and have it in abundance (John 10:10).

When we glorify God, we honor God for our life and for the lives of others. We honor God by trusting God with our lives that really belong to Him. We are not our own for we were bought with a price. Proverbs 3:5–6 (NLT) says, *"Trust in the Lord with all your heart; do not depend on your own understanding. Seek his will in all you do, and he will show you which path to take."* The God who gave us life can be trusted to direct our lives. It is glorifying God that puts us in position to receive blessings from God (1 Samuel 2:30).

IN SEARCH OF A TREASURED LIFE

List three things you are now doing or can commit to start doing this week to glorify or honor God:

1. _____.

2. _____.

3. _____.

"…Whatever you do, do it all for the glory of God"
—1 Corinthians 10:31b (NIV)

Think about one thing that has already happened in your life that could have been different if you had applied this Scripture to it, and write it in the following sentence:

My decision to _____

could have been a different one with a different outcome if I had focused

on glorifying God rather than _____.

RELATED SCRIPTURES ABOUT GLORIFYING GOD

(If you want to read more about what the Bible says about **glorifying God**, here are some related Scriptures. You may find others in your Bible reading. If you do, add them to the list.)

Psalm 50:23
John 12:26; 21:19
1 Peter 2:12

COINS FOR YOUR TREASURE CHEST

(Entries in this section are additional quotes from other sources or thoughts written by the author. If you find more quotes on this topic, please add them along with the source of the quote.)

"…Our purpose should be to display the glory of God in human life; to live a life 'hidden with Christ in God' in our everyday human conditions (Colossians 3:31)."
—Oswald Chambers, *My Utmost for His Highest* (11/16)

"No matter where life's road takes us, we have to make the right choices, and do the right thing—Glorify God through our life."
—"Glorify God/life and truth," Pinterest/Sayings
and "God" in pinterest.com

HUMILITY

"Humility is the solid foundation of all the virtues."
—Confucius

YOUR LIFE IS TO BE TREASURED. LIVE A LIFE OF **HUMILITY**
THAT GLORIFIES GOD AND NOT YOURSELF.

 KEY SCRIPTURE

True humility and fear of the Lord lead to riches, honor, and long life.
—Proverbs 22:4 (NLT)

Humility is the state of not being proud, arrogant, or aggressive. It is strength under control. To be humble is to be meek (not necessarily weak) and to portray a spirit of modesty. It means that we do not think more highly of ourselves than we ought to think. When we are humble, we have a proper perspective of our vertical relationship with God and a horizontal relationship with those we can serve. *"So humble yourselves under the mighty power of God, and at the right time he will lift you up in honor"* (1 Peter 5:6, NLT).

When God has pre-eminence in both our natural and spiritual lives, we are less likely to become victims and casualties of pride. *"Pride gives the evil one a key to our lives. Humility changes the lock and gives God the key when we openly admit that we need God and seek God's forgiveness for our sins. No proud person can do this"* (Gilbert and Ronald A. Beers, *Touchpoints Bible Promises*). Proverbs 22:4 emphasizes that God will give abundance, recognition, and life to those who are humble.

IN SEARCH OF A TREASURED LIFE

On a scale of 1–5, with 5 being the highest, how humble are you? _____

At this present level of humility, do you find it easy or difficult to glorify God while serving others? Explain.

_____

_____

_____

_____

_____

What can you do to change your present situation for the better? I can ...

_____

_____

_____

_____

_____.

"When you do things, do not let selfish pride be your guide. Instead, be humble and give more honor to others than to yourselves. Do not be interested only in your own life, but be interested in the lives of others. In your lives, you must think and act like Christ Jesus.
—Philippians 2:3–5 (NCV)

What would be different about your life if you practiced the humility of Christ in your daily interactions with others?

_____

_____

_____

_____

_____

RELATED SCRIPTURES ABOUT HUMILITY

(If you want to read more about what the Bible says about **humility**, here are some related Scriptures. You may find others in your Bible reading. If you do, add them to the list.)

Psalm 138:6; 149:4
Proverbs 3:34; 25:6–7; 27:23
Isaiah 29:19
Daniel 10:12
Matthew 18:4; 23:11–12
I Peter 5:6–7

COINS FOR YOUR TREASURE CHEST

(Entries in this section are additional quotes from other sources or thoughts written by the author. If you find more quotes on this topic, please add them along with the source of the quote.)

"Humility comes before honor."
—Proverbs 15:33(b) (NIV)

"God opposes the proud, but gives grace to the humble."
—James 4:6(b) (NIV)

9

INVESTMENT

Your life is to be treasured.
INVEST *now in your future.*

 **KEY SCRIPTURE**

Commit to the Lord whatever you do, and your plans will succeed.
—Proverbs 16:3 (NIV)

An **investment** in your future begins with believing within yourself that you are capable of becoming all that God created and intended you to be. There should be a sense of urgency in how we live our lives if only because tomorrow is not promised to anyone. That being said, we still need to invest our time, talents, and energy in becoming all that God intended and created us to be. To invest in your future means to make a commitment to living your life in a manner that pleases God. Pleasing God puts you in line to be blessed by God. To commit to God is to invest in the lifestyle that God calls you to live.

Treasuring life by investing in your future does not mean making a commitment to things that may only guarantee financial or material gain. In his Sermon on the Mount, Jesus makes a clear distinction between "earthly" and "heavenly" treasures (Matthew 6:19–21). The main goal of life should not be to accumulate material things. These things can be lost, ruined, destroyed or stolen. More importantly, over-emphasis on material things can destroy our heart and mind.

It is a fact that we need food, clothing, and shelter to live. While we need material things to live, the main goal of life should be to invest in living in a way that seeks a personal relationship with God. If you want to make a sound investment in your future today, begin by trusting God with a heart that obeys God, and live according to the Word of God. When we acknowledge, appreciate, and honor God in all that we say and do, the Bible affirms that God will direct our paths (Proverbs 3:5–6).

IN SEARCH OF A TREASURED LIFE

Keep a daily journal for one week of your activities by writing down the activities that occupy your time from the time you get up until the time you go to bed. A **journal** is a written record of events or activities that one keeps for personal use. You can list things like school, work, time spent with family and friends, watching TV, etc. Remember to keep it simple.

- Get a composition notebook.
- Write the day of the week and the date on each page for seven days.
- Divide each page in half with a vertical line down the center of the page from top to bottom.

- On the left of the page, record the time in 30 minute intervals from the time you wake up until the time you go to bed.
- On the right side of the center line write your routine or activity corresponding to the time on the left.

For example:

Monday   [Date]

6:30 a.m.	Wake up and get ready for school or work
7:00 a.m.	Eat breakfast
7:30 a.m.	Leave for school or work

This should be a pretty accurate record of what you generally do each day. Look at your activities and highlight the times you feel you are investing in your future.

Are you doing at least one thing each day that will help you later in achieving your future goals in life?
Check one: ( ) Yes   ( ) No   ( ) I'm not sure of my goals.

"For I know the plans I have for you, declares the Lord, plans to prosper you and not harm you, plans to give you a hope and a future."
—Jeremiah 29:11 (NIV)

After reading and reflecting on the Scripture printed above, answer the following questions.
- What plans do you now have for your immediate (this year) or distant (five to ten years from now) future?

_____

_____

_____

- Do you think that God has the same plans for you?
  Select one: ( ) Yes   ( ) No   ( ) Maybe   ( ) I have no idea

- What can you do now, at this stage in your life, to become aligned with God's plans "to prosper you and not harm you—to give you hope and a future"?

_____

_____

_____

RELATED SCRIPTURES ABOUT INVESTMENT

(If you want to read more about what the Bible says about **investment**, here are some related Scriptures. You may find others in your Bible reading. If you do, add them to the list.)

John 6:27
Romans 2:7
1 Corinthians 13:7
Galatians 6:9
2 Timothy 2:3, 10–12
Hebrews 10:36; 11:27; 12:1–3
James 1:12; 5:11
1 Peter 1:25; 4:13

COINS FOR YOUR TREASURE CHEST

(Entries in this section are additional quotes from other sources or thoughts written by the author. If you find more quotes on this topic, please add them along with the source of the quote.)

"To seek God and His kingdom is the greatest investment we can ever make in this life."
—*My Daily Psalms and Prayers* (03/16)

"Life isn't about finding yourself. Life is about creating yourself."
—George Bernard Shaw

"The highest reward for a person's toil is not what they get for it, but what they become by it."
—John Ruskin

JOYFULNESS

"One of the most tragic things I know about human nature is that all of us tend to put off living. We are all dreaming of some magical rose garden over the horizon—instead of enjoying the roses that are blooming outside our window today."
—Dale Carnegie

Your life is to be treasured. Be **JOYFUL** *for every day of life that God gives you.*

 KEY SCRIPTURE

Be full of joy in the Lord always. I will say again, be full of joy....
And God's peace, which is so great we cannot understand it,
will keep your hearts and minds in Christ Jesus.
—Philippians 4:4, 6 (NCV)

Joyfulness is showing happiness, delight, or gladness for what is, or for what one expects will be. Pure joy is finding peace with God. God's word should be the source of our joy and our peace. True joy can only come from having a thankful heart and from living a life that glorifies God who created you. It comes from living a life in humble devotion to God. Only after we find joy in ourselves can we find joy in the lives of others. Living a godly life results in a treasured life illumined by God's presence and filled with unspeakable joy.

The situations or challenges we face in life do not define us. We are defined by how we handle them because we are free to choose our attitudes and our moods. We must learn to find happiness in the rhythms of our daily lives. Joy, for those who follow Christ does not depend on circumstances, but in knowing what Christ has done for us (1Thessalonians 5:16). When we choose to begin each day of our lives with joyfulness, we can focus on the positive rather than the negative.

Our cups are half-full rather than half-empty. We can be *"more than conquerors through Him who loves us"* (Romans 8:37). If we choose to begin each day by walking in the light of God's presence, the joy of the Lord will be our strength (Nehemiah 8:10).

Recipe for Happiness

2 Heaping Cups of **Patience**
1 Heart full of **Love**
2 Hands full of **Generosity**
A Dash of **Laughter**
1 Head full of **Understanding**
Sprinkle generously with **Kindness**.
Add plenty of **Faith** and mix well.
Spread over a period of a lifetime,
And **Serve** everyone you meet.
—Author Unknown

🔍 IN SEARCH OF A TREASURED LIFE

What makes you joyful for your life? Check all that apply to you:

___ (a) spending time with family and friends

___ (b) spending time alone with God

___ (c) being active

___ (d) eating my favorite food or dessert

___ (e) Other _____

When you need help changing your attitude about your life, who or what helps you find joy and look on the brighter side? Check all that apply:

___ (a) my parents

___ (b) a close friend

___ (c) my teacher or coach

___ (d) Someone less fortunate than I am

___ (e) Other _____

Give the person who helps you find joy a call, write them a thank-you note, send them an email, text or tweet thanking them for their encouragement).

RELATED SCRIPTURES ABOUT JOYFULNESS

(If you want to read more about what the Bible says about **joyfulness**, here are some related Scriptures. You may find others in your Bible reading. If you do, add them to the list.)

Psalm 64:10; 97:11; 100:1–5

Isaiah 55:12; 61:10

Habakkuk 3:17–18

1 Thessalonians 5:15

James 1:2

COINS FOR YOUR TREASURE CHEST

(Entries in this section are additional quotes from other sources or thoughts written by the author. If you find more quotes on this topic, please add them along with the source of the quote.)

"The prescription for joyful living is very simple:
If you want to be happy, treat people right."
—Robert Schuller, *Pearls of Power*

"In all of living, have much fun and laughter.
Life is to be enjoyed, not just endured."
—Z. Gordon B. Hinckley

"God designed you for happiness. He created you to be joyful and fully alive.
The gift of Almighty God to us is life."
—Dr. Norman Vincent Peale, *Guideposts Outreach Publications* (Joy)

KINDNESS

"I expect to pass through this life but once. If therefore, there be any kindness I can show, or good thing I can do to any fellow being, let me do it now, and not defer or neglect it, as I shall not pass this way again."
—William Penn

YOUR LIFE IS TO BE TREASURED. SHOW **KINDNESS** TO OTHERS WHO SHARE THIS WORLD WITH YOU. TREAT OTHERS AS YOU WOULD LIKE TO BE TREATED.

 KEY SCRIPTURE

Be kind and compassionate to one another, forgiving each other, just as in Christ God forgave you.—Ephesians 4:32 (NIV)

Kindness is the quality or state of being kind, agreeable, considerate, gentle or gracious. It is a fruit of the Spirit and one of the Christian virtues. (See Galatians 5:22.) To be kind is to show an unselfish concern for others and their well-being. To be kind is to treat others as you wish to be treated. In reality, however, it is impossible to be kind to others if you are not kind to yourself. In this respect, kindness is like love. How can you love others if you do not love yourself? If you treasure your life, you will first of all, be kind to yourself, and will then taking advantage of every opportunity to show kindness toward others. Someone has said that "kindness grows the spirit and strengthens the soul."

In Ephesians 4:32, the Apostle Paul links kindness with compassion (tenderheartedness) and forgiveness. This is what God graciously did for us through His Son, Jesus Christ. Our salvation is the result of God's mercy (kindness) and grace. When we are kind to ourselves and others, we receive and accept God's grace. In doing this, we honor God.

$\mathcal{Q}$ IN SEARCH OF A TREASURED LIFE

"Make sure that nobody pays back wrong for wrong, but always try to be kind to each other and to everyone else" —1Thessalonians 5:15 (NIV)

Getting even is never a good option for anyone, especially for those who are believers in Christ. Think of something that you are holding onto with intentions of getting even with someone. What will it take for you to forgive him or her and show kindness instead?
Select one:
___ (a) an apology
___ (b) a bribe
___ (c) a promise not to do it again
___ (d) I won't ever let go
___ (e) Other _____

How does holding on to a grudge (wanting to get even with a person) make you feel inside? Select one:
___ (a) great
___ (b) Now, we're even
___ (c) all balled up inside
___ (d) unhappy
___ (e) Other_____

What effect do you think holding a grudge against someone has on that person? Select one:

___ (a) They could care less

___ (b) unhappy

___ (c) They have no clue that I have something against them

___ (d) Other _____

4. If you chose in a particular situation to be kind to someone without expecting anything in return, describe in a few sentences how this made you feel.

_____

_____

_____

_____

RELATED SCRIPTURES ABOUT KINDNESS

(If you want to read more about what the Bible says about **kindness**, here are some related Scriptures. You may find others in your Bible reading. If you do, add them to the list.)

Proverbs 11:17; 12:25; 14:30, 31

Jeremiah 9:24

Luke 6:35

Romans 11:22

Galatians 5:22

Ephesians 2:7

2 Timothy 2:24

Titus 3:3–7

2 Peter 1:5–9

COINS FOR YOUR TREASURE CHEST

(Entries in this section are additional quotes from other sources or thoughts written by the author. If you find more quotes on this topic, please add them along with the source of the quote.)

"The words of kindness are more healing to a drooping heart than balm or honey."—Sarah Fielding

"You must give time to your fellowman—even if it's a little thing, do something for others, something for which you get no pay, but the privilege of doing it."
—Albert Schweitzer

LOVE

*"Of all earthly music, that which reaches farthest into heaven
is the beating of a truly loving heart."*
—Henry Ward Beecher

YOUR LIFE IS TO BE TREASURED. **LOVE** *GOD WITH ALL YOUR HEART,
AND* **LOVE** *OTHERS AS YOU* **LOVE** *YOURSELF.*

KEY SCRIPTURE

*Love is patient, and kind. Love is not jealous or boastful or proud or rude.
It does not demand its own way. It is not irritable, and keeps no record of being
wronged. It does not rejoice about injustice but rejoices whenever the truth
comes out. Love never gives up, never loses faith, is always hopeful,
and endures through every circumstance.*
—1 Corinthians 13:4–7 (NLT)

Love is unselfish loyalty and kind concern for the good of another. The four verses above, from what is usually referred to as the "love chapter" (1 Corinthians 13), capture the true nature and motive of love from the Christian's perspective. We are taught to love by the Father in 1John 4:19, by the Son in John 13:34, and by the Holy Spirit in Romans 5:5. One distinguishing trait of a true believer in Christ is love for others as Christ loved us, and as we love ourselves. Our standard for love, then, is the one set and modeled by Jesus Christ (John 13:34–35).

In the first place, we are born to love because the God who gave us life is love. God, out of love, sent His only Son to the world, and the Son gave His life for us on Calvary's cross. As a result of Christ's dying for our sins, anyone who believes in Him by faith is promised everlasting life. The Bible expresses the greatest act of love this way:

"For God loved the world so much that he gave his one and only Son, so that everyone who believes in him will not perish but have eternal life" (John 3:16, NLT).

Of *faith, hope* and *love,* the greatest is **love** (1 Corinthians 13:13) because love is the motive underlying all that God has done, is doing, and will do according to His Word. It is love that is the eyes of faith and the heart of hope. If you treasure your life, you will first of all love God completely. You will then be able to love others unconditionally. It is loving God and yourself that gives you the capacity to love your neighbor. In many cases, your neighbor may not look like you or share the same values that you have.

Life is for caring and sharing without qualifications, stipulations, or reservations. A treasured life is a life where one seeks to be the best that God created them to be. This is done in large measure through love. According to the apostle Paul, love is *"…a way of life that is best of all"* (1 Corinthians 12:31, NLT).

🔍 IN SEARCH OF A TREASURED LIFE

Who do you feel it is most difficult for you to love at this point in your life as love is described in 1 Corinthians 13? Select one:

___ (a) God

___ (b) yourself

___ (c) a family member, friend, or neighbor who lives near you

___ (d) someone you really don't personally know

___ (d) Other _____   _____

Explain in two or three sentences why you find it difficult to love this person.

_____

_____

_____

_____

_____

_____

_____.

Read and reflect on Matthew 22:37–40.

What is one thing you can do today to help you to be obedient to Jesus' commandment to love the person you find it difficult to love right now?

_____

_____

_____

_____.

RELATED SCRIPTURES ABOUT LOVE

(If you want to read more about what the Bible says about **love**, here are some related Scriptures. You may find others in your Bible reading. If you do, add them to the list.)

Deuteronomy 7:9; 11:13–15

Psalms 37:4; 91:14; 145:20

Proverbs 8:17

1 Corinthians 2:9; 10:24; 14:1

Ephesians 1:4; 5:1–2

1Timothy 1:5

Hebrews 13:1

1 Peter 1:22; 4:8

1 John 2:5; 3:1–3, 11–14, 18; 4:10

2 John 3, 5, 6

COINS FOR YOUR TREASURE CHEST

(Entries in this section are additional quotes from other sources or thoughts written by the author. If you find more quotes on this topic, please add them along with the source of the quote.)

"If there is anything better than to be loved, it is in loving."—Anonymous

"Love is the common denominator to life; the magic potion of the soul."
—Dennis Kimbro, *What Keeps Me Standing*, p. 145

MODERATION

"Everything that exceeds the bounds of moderation has an unstable foundation."—Seneca

---

*Y*OUR LIFE IS TO BE TREASURED. *L*IVE A LIFE OF
MODERATION *WITH TEMPERANCE IN ALL THAT YOU DO.*

 KEY SCRIPTURE

Let everyone see that you are considerate in all that you do.
Remember the Lord is coming soon.
—Philippians 4:5 (NLT)

Moderation is the act of being calm, temperate, or of avoiding extreme acts of behavior. When you live your life within the boundaries of reasonableness and restraint, the likelihood of violent behavior or uncontrollable conflict is diminished. Moderation is self-control. It is a key to not only longevity, but also to balance in your life. It is indispensable for those who are truly happy with themselves as God created them, and are good stewards of the life that God has given them.

IN SEARCH OF A TREASURED LIFE

How reasonable and considerate are you in your interactions with others?
Select one:

___ (a) very

___ (b) somewhat

___ (c) very little

___ (d) not enough

___ (e) not at all

How do you feel about your response to this question?

_____

_____

_____

_____

RELATED SCRIPTURES ABOUT MODERATION

(If you want to read more about what the Bible says about **moderation**, here are some related Scriptures. You may find others in your Bible reading. If you do, add them to the list.)

Psalm 39:1–2
Proverbs 16:32; 25:28; 29:11
Galatians 5:22–23
James 1:19–20
1 Peter 1:13
2 Peter 1:5–7

COINS FOR YOUR TREASURE CHEST

(Entries in this section are additional quotes from other sources or thoughts written by the author. If you find more quotes on this topic, please add them along with the source of the quote.)

"The pursuit of even the best things ought to be calm and tranquil."
—Cicero

NAME

"Names have a meaning. Names have a history. Wrapped up in a person's name is who he is, what family she came from, and how God has blessed that particular family by his grace in a particular manner."
—Jeremiah Wright, *What Makes You So Strong*

YOUR LIFE IS TO BE TREASURED. STRIVE TO HAVE A GOOD **NAME** *AND REPUTATION BECAUSE YOUR NAME HAS MEANING AND VALUE.*

 KEY SCRIPTURE

Choose a good reputation over great riches;
being held in high esteem is better than silver or gold.
—Proverbs 22:1 (NLT)

If you don't think that your name has importance, think again. Your **name** is much more than what people call you. It is also the reputation you establish with others. The writer of Proverbs 22:1 advises us to measure our lives by our reputation rather than our riches. This is where one finds the real treasure. Having a good name (character) is more valuable than great wealth. All the money in the world cannot buy happiness or a good name.

Your name is an introduction to who you really are beyond what others can readily see. There is a reason your parents gave you the name that they did. Finding out the reason for or the story behind your name could be a key to unlocking the hopes, aspirations, dreams, and expectations your parents had for you when you were born.

$\mathcal{Q}$ IN SEARCH OF A TREASURED LIFE

Talk to your parents and other family members about the history of your name. What did you discover about the reason your parents named you as they did? Were you named after someone in the Bible, your family, a historical person, a well-known sports figure or someone else?
Jot notes here about what you learn:

_____

_____

_____

_____.

What value can knowing the history of your name have in your life as you go forward?

_____

_____

_____

_____.

Rate your reputation in the following areas of your life as good, fair, less than favorable:

- Your Faith _____
- Your Family _____
- Your Friends _____
- Your School _____
- Your Job_____
- Other (_____) _____

What is one thing you can do now to improve your reputation in the areas above where improvement is needed?

I can:

_____

_____

_____

_____.

RELATED SCRIPTURES ABOUT YOUR NAME (REPUTATION)

(If you want to read more about what the Bible says about your **name (reputation)**, here are some related Scriptures. You may find others in your Bible reading. If you do, add them to the list.)

Proverbs 3:3–4
Isaiah 49:14–16
Zephaniah 3:20
Romans 14:17–18
Philippians 2:9–11; 4:4–5
Hebrews 11:39

COINS FOR YOUR TREASURE CHEST

(Entries in this section are additional quotes from other sources or thoughts written by the author. If you find more quotes on this topic, please add them along with the source of the quote.)

"A name is a kind of face whereby one is known.—Thomas Fuller

OPPORTUNITY

"To improve the golden moment of opportunity and catch the good that is within reach, is the great art of life."
—Samuel Johnson

YOUR LIFE IS TO BE TREASURED. TAKE ADVANTAGE OF EVERY **OPPORTUNITY** *YOU HAVE TO MAKE A DIFFERENCE IN THE WORLD AND TO MAKE YOUR LIFE COUNT.*

 KEY SCRIPTURE

To those who use well what they are given, even more will be given, and they will have an abundance. But from those who do nothing, even what little they have will be taken away.
—Matthew 25:29 (NLT)

To have **opportunity** means that there is a good chance through some endeavor for personal benefit, progress, or success. Opportunity is a favorable or suitable situation. Jesus says in Matthew 25:29 that God honors and rewards those who are faithful enough to take full advantage of the opportunities that He provides. When we trust and obey God and follow Christ, we are entering into a relationship with God where nothing will prevent us from fulfilling our destiny. Let your steps be ordered by the Word of God. His word will be a lamp for your feet and a light for your path (Psalm 119:105).

Although there will be times in our lives when we recall missed opportunities, failure to accept God's saving grace should not be one of them. The greatest opportunity of a lifetime that each of us has is the opportunity to accept Christ and be saved. John 3:16–17, quoted earlier in this book, affirms not only God's love for us, but also the opportunity we have to be saved by believing in Jesus. Taking advantage of the opportunity to know Christ as our personal Lord and Savior opens the door to a treasured life. This is an opportunity that should not be missed.

IN SEARCH OF A TREASURED LIFE

Are you hesitant about pursuing an opportunity that you currently have?
Check one: ( ) Yes   ( ) No

Read and meditate on the Scriptures at the end of this section and pray to God, according to his will, in Jesus' name by the power of the Holy Spirit for discernment and guidance. Remember this: *"Where God guides, He provides."*

Share your feelings with a friend about an opportunity that you thought was really meant for you, but of which you did not take advantage. What lesson or lessons did you learn?
I learned:

_____

_____

_____

_____.

RELATED SCRIPTURES ABOUT OPPORTUNITY

(If you want to read more about what the Bible says about **opportunity**, here are some related Scriptures. You may find others in your Bible reading. If you do, add them to the list.)

Joshua 1:7–9

Isaiah 55:6–7

Matthew 13:17–23

John 9:4

Ephesians 5:15–20

Philippians 4:13

Hebrews 4:1–7

Revelation 3:8, 20

Hebrews 11:39

COINS FOR YOUR TREASURE CHEST

(Entries in this section are additional quotes from other sources or thoughts written by the author. If you find more quotes on this topic, please add them along with the source of the quote.)

"God's opportunities conform to his word. Anything that contradicts God's word is not an opportunity from God."
—V. Gilbert Beers & Ronald A. Beers, *Touch Points Bible Promises*

"Nothing is worse than missing an opportunity that could have changed your life."—goodlifequotation.com

"See every day as an opportunity to better yourself."—pictureqoutes.com

PURPOSE

"Life isn't about finding yourself; it's about discovering who God created you to be.
—Sayings about Life and Life Purpose on Pinterest

"Keep on asking, and you will receive what you ask for. Keep on seeking and you will find. Keep on knocking and the door will be opened to you. For everyone who asks receives. Everyone who seeks, finds. And to everyone who knocks, the door will be opened."
—Matthew 7:7–8 (NLT)

YOUR LIFE IS TO BE TREASURED. SEEK TO FIND YOUR TRUE **PURPOSE** *IN LIFE.*

 KEY SCRIPTURE

You can make many plans, but the Lord's purpose will prevail.
—Proverbs 19:21 (NLT)

Purpose is the reason for doing something. It is the goal, objective, or aim to which we aspire in life. Some of the Scriptures in the Bible emphasize that a life with meaning is one that is aligned with God's purpose for our lives. Knowing God's purpose for us gives our lives meaning. How can we know God's purpose for our lives? To know God's purpose for our lives requires that we read, meditate upon, pray about, and practice living according to God's word. The power of prayer should not be underestimated when we ask God to reveal his plans for our lives. Equally important, we should patiently wait for God's response. Waiting patiently for God to reveal his purpose for our lives shows our trust and dependence upon his word.

In our quest for a purposeful life, we will face many challenges, but it is important to remember that finding our true purpose in life is greater than any obstacle we may face along the way.

When we live free from feeling a need to be in control of every aspect of our lives, we can become who God created us to be. We can live the treasured life that God intended for us to live when we remember that it is God who is in total control, not us. Patiently wait for God to guide you down the path he has already chosen for your life.

IN SEARCH OF A TREASURED LIFE

In a few words, write down what you know or feel that your purpose is in the life God has given you.

_____

_____

_____

_____

_____.

Select the response that best describes where you are now in your life: When it comes to praying for God to reveal his purpose for my life...

____ (a) I'm all into praying for God's guidance.

____ (b) I've gone down this road before and it hasn't helped yet.

____ (c) I really don't know how to pray.

____ (d) I don't think God really cares about me.

____ (e) Other _____

Write the name of a family member, friend or someone from the faith community who can help you with your prayer life:

_____

Ask this person for help in praying to understand God's purpose for your life.

Select the statement that best describes your level of patience today in seeking to find your purpose in life:

____ (a) I'm at my wit's end.

____ (b) I'm patiently waiting for God to show me.

____ (c) I've taken matters into my own hands.

____ (d) It's too late. I've given up hope.

____ (e) Other_____.

RELATED SCRIPTURES ABOUT PURPOSE

(If you want to read more about what the Bible says about **purpose**, here are some related Scriptures. You may find others in your Bible reading. If you do, add them to the list.)

Genesis 1:26

Exodus 9:16

Proverbs 20:5

Ecclesiastes 12:13

Jeremiah 29:11–13

Micah 6:8

Acts 1:8; 20:24

Romans 12:1

Ephesians 2:10

Philippians 2:12–13

2 Timothy 1:9

James 1:18

2 Peter 1:10–11

COINS FOR YOUR TREASURE CHEST

(Entries in this section are additional quotes from other sources or thoughts written by the author. If you find more quotes on this topic, please add them along with the source of the quote.)

"If you're alive, there's a purpose for your life."
—Rick Warren

"Prayer is a binding necessity in the lives of men and nations."
—Alexis Carrell

"The purpose of human life is to serve and show compassion and the will to help others."
—Albert Schweitzer

"Have patience with all things, but first of all with yourself."
—Francis De Sales, *www.VeryBestQuotes.com*

"Patience is power; with time and patience the mulberry leaf becomes silk."
—Chinese Proverb

QUIETNESS

"The good and the wise lead quiet lives"
—Euripides

YOUR LIFE IS TO BE TREASURED. IN MOMENTS OF **QUIETNESS**,
FOCUS ON LIVING A QUIET AND PEACEABLE LIFE OF MEDITATION, DEVOTION,
PRAYER, REFLECTION AND PURPOSE.

 KEY SCRIPTURE

And the work of righteousness shall be peace; and the effect of
righteousness quietness and assurance forever.—Isaiah 32:17 (KJV)

Quietness is a state of being calm, relaxed and free from noise or distraction. Though quietness can seem to be passive in nature, its benefits can be productive and positive. It depends upon what one does during periods of being quiet. The Apostle Paul says in 1Thessalonians 4:11 that one should *"make it a goal to live a quiet life, minding your own business…."* One way to do this is to follow the advice the Psalmist gives in Psalm 1 for living a happy (blessed) life. This person does not follow the advice of those with evil intent, or align themselves with those who do wrong or belittle others. Their delight comes from obeying the word of God and meditating on God's word daily.

Quietness provides both the atmosphere and opportunity for listening for God and focusing on the important things in life. It is a time to be still while being attuned to hearing from God, being sustained by God, and being empowered by God. It is good for us to do this because it also pleases God our Father.

If quietness in one's life is fueled by withdrawal or separation from our faith, family, and friends, that could be a devastating position in which to be. However, sometimes in our lives with its twists and turns, we do find ourselves separated from God, our family, and our friends. It is during these periods in our lives that we must remember the words of God in Isaiah 30:15: *"Only in returning to me and resting in me will you be saved. In quietness and confidence is your strength"* (NLT). God promises that by returning to and trusting in him, we can be saved and strengthened in quietness (peace) and confidence. A treasured life is one where in quietness our attention invariably turns to God.

In Isaiah 32:17, righteousness is said to be a precursor to peace, for righteousness works to bring peace. It results in quietness and assurance. If we would learn and apply the discipline of quietness in our lives, we would do well to practice righteous living. Jesus expresses this point another way in Matthew 6:33: *"Seek the kingdom of God above all else, and live righteously, and he will give you everything you need"* (NLT).

IN SEARCH OF A TREASURED LIFE

How much quiet time (in minutes) do you spend daily in prayer and meditation, alone with God? _____.
(If you kept a journal for a week as suggested in the chapter on **Investment**, look back at your typical week. Do you pray to God when you get up in the morning and before you go to bed at night? If you do, write the minutes devoted to morning and evening prayer in the blank space above.)

Do you think the quiet time you are currently spending with God is enough?
Check one: ( ) Yes   ( ) No

If your answer is "no" how can you possibly reorganize your day to gain more quiet time with God?

_____

_____

_____

_____

_____

_____

RELATED SCRIPTURES ABOUT QUIETNESS

(If you want to read more about what the Bible says about **quietness**, here are some related Scriptures. You may find others in your Bible reading. If you do, add them to the list.)

Job 34:29
Proverbs 11:12
Ecclesiastes 4:6
Matthew 6:56; 14:23
Mark 1:35; 6:31
Luke 4:42; 5:16
2 Thessalonians 3:12
1Timothy 2:1–2
1 Peter 3:4

COINS FOR YOUR TREASURE CHEST

(Entries in this section are additional quotes from other sources or thoughts written by the author. If you find more quotes on this topic, please add them along with the source of the quote.)

"Spending quiet time with God can bring quiet rest from God"
—*Our Daily Bread,* August 17, 2013

"To have a quiet mind is to possess one mind wholly;
to have a calm spirit is to command one's self."
—Hamilton Wright Mabie

"Our greatest experiences are our quietest moments."
—Friedrich Nietzsche, *livinglifefully.com*

"Quiet the mind, and the soul will speak."
—Ma Jaya Sati Bhagavali, *okyDay.com*

RESPECT

"Respect yourself enough to walk away from anything that no longer serves you, grows you, or makes you happy."
—Author Unknown

YOUR LIFE IS TO BE TREASURED. **RESPECT** *YOUR LIFE AND THE LIVES OF OTHERS JUST AS YOU HAVE HONOR AND* **RESPECT** *FOR GOD.*

 KEY SCRIPTURE

Respect everyone. Love your Christian brothers and sisters. Fear God, and respect the king.
—1 Peter 2:17 (NLT)

Respect s the act of having consideration for others as well as one's self. It is holding others in high regard or esteem. When we show disrespect for others, it could be that we suffer from a lack of self-respect. If your life has little or no meaning to you, how can you respect someone else's life? More importantly, having respect for ourselves and others is virtually impossible if we have no respect for the One who gave us life.

Our respect for God means that we love, trust, obey, and honor God for who He is, for what He has done, for what He is doing, and for what the Word of God promises that He will do in our lives. We can have a deeper appreciation for the gift of life when we have appreciation and respect for the giver of life. From a Christian perspective, respect implies that we should be exemplary citizens so that God will be glorified (1 Peter 2:11–17). Love for God and for our neighbor means that we respect and are being obedient to God's commandment. Love does what is right and just and seeks the best for others.

IN SEARCH OF A TREASURED LIFE

Who do you have the most respect for at this time in your life? (Select one.)
____ (a) My parents
____ (b) My elders
____ (c) Myself
____ (d) Relatives
____ (e) Friends
____ (f) other _____.

What persons or groups of people do you have the least amount of respect for at this time in your life and why?

_____

_____

Select your response to the following statements:

• My respect for God at this time in my life is
____ (a) just about right
____ (b) not what it should be

___ (c) growing each day

___ (d) I'm not sure

___ (e) other _____.

- My respect for myself at this time in my life is

___ (a) sorely lacking

___ (b) off the charts

___ (c) pretty good

___ (d) better than it used to be

___ (e) other _____.

- My respect for others at this time in my life is

___ (a) okay, if they respect me

___ (b) not as good as it should be

___ (c) pretty good right now

___ (d) It's all about me, baby!

___ (e) Other _____.

In a few words, write down your thoughts about what you feel you can do to improve the level of respect you have for God, others, and yourself.

To improve my level of respect for God, I can

_____

_____

To improve my level of respect for myself, I can

_____

_____

To improve my level of respect for others, I can

_____

_____

RELATED SCRIPTURES ABOUT RESPECT

(If you want to read more about what the Bible says about **respect**, here are some related Scriptures. You may find others in your Bible reading. If you do, add them to the list.)

Leviticus 19:3, 32

2 Kings 13:23

Psalm 40:4; 138:6

Proverbs 11:6

Isaiah 17:7

Malachi 1:6

Romans 13:1–7

Ephesians 5:33; 6:5

1 Thessalonians 4:12; 5:12

1 Timothy 3:4, 8, 11; 6:1

Titus 2:2, 7

1 Peter 3:7, 16

COINS FOR YOUR TREASURE CHEST

(Entries in this section are additional quotes from other sources or thoughts written by the author. If you find more quotes on this topic, please add them along with the source of the quote.)

"Respect is not imposed nor begged. It's earned and offered."
—Author unknown

"How you carry yourself, what you stand for—that's how you gain respect."
—Mildred Taylor

"It's always been a mystery to me how people can respect themselves when they humiliate other people."
—Mahatma Gandhi

*"Respect is having **Reverence** for God, **Empathy** for others, standing in **Solidarity** with them, having **Patience**, providing **Encouragement**, **Compassion**, and being **Tolerant** of those who do not share your God, ideas, or values."*

STANDARDS

*"It is not hard to make decisions
once you know what your values are."*
—Roy E. Disney

YOUR LIFE IS TO BE TREASURED. HAVE **STANDARDS** *BY WHICH YOU LIVE.
YOU CAN LEARN THESE AT HOME, AT CHURCH, AND AT SCHOOL.*

 KEY SCRIPTURE

*Hold to the standard of sound teaching that you have heard from me,
in the faith and love that are in Christ Jesus.*
—2 Timothy 1:13 (HCSB)

Standards are moral, ethical codes that allow one to tell the difference between right and wrong. They are ideas or principles by which we live. Standards are our core values, and form the moral compass leading us to live a principled life. How does one get standards by which to live? You can learn these at home, in school, and in church.

The standards or values that are important to living a treasured life are in many ways contradictory to the worldly values of prestige, power, pleasure, wealth or fame. Instead, the Bible teaches us the important values to have in living a life that pleases God. We must seek joy and happiness within the boundaries of God's moral standards. These standards include, among others, kindness and respect for all people, humility, honesty, generosity, self-control, and forgiveness. This is what Christ modeled and what He taught.

IN SEARCH OF A TREASURED LIFE

After giving it some thought, what are the top three standards or values by which you are living today?

(1) _____

(2) _____

(3) _____

Of the three standards you listed above, which one is the most important to you? Why?

_____

_____

_____

_____

_____.

RELATED SCRIPTURES ABOUT STANDARDS

(If you want to read more about what the Bible says about **standards**, here are some related Scriptures. You may find others in your Bible reading. If you do, add them to the list.)

Matthew 6:24; 20:25–28
Romans 2:5–11; 6:17
2 Timothy 3:14
Titus 1:9, 13; 2:1, 2
1 John 2:16

COINS FOR YOUR TREASURE CHEST

(Entries in this section are additional quotes from other sources or thoughts written by the author. If you find more quotes on this topic, please add them along with the source of the quote.)

"The ultimate source of a happy life is the attention we pay to our inner values."
—Dalai Lama

"Keep your thoughts positive because your thoughts become your words.
Keep your words positive because your words become your behavior.
Keep your behavior positive because your behavior becomes your habits.
Keep your habits positive because your habits become your values.
Keep your values positive because your values become your destiny."
—Mahatma Gandhi

TIME

"Time is so fleeting that if we do not remember God in our youth,
age may find us incapable of thinking about him."
—Hans Christian Anderson

YOUR LIFE IS TO BE TREASURED. USE YOUR **TIME** *WISELY AS A GIFT FROM GOD.*

 KEY SCRIPTURE

So be very careful how you live. Do not live like those who are unwise, but live
wisely. Use every chance you have for doing good because these are evil times.
So do not be foolish, but learn what the Lord wants you to do.
—Ephesians 5:15–17 (NLT)

Time can be categorized as "past," "present," or "future." We measure time in seconds, minutes, hours, days, weeks, months, and years. Time is a sequence of events that have already occurred, beginning from one's birth (the past). It is a sequence of actions and events that are occurring now, even as this is being read (the present). Time is also a sequence or series of actions and events that will occur in whatever moments we have left on this earth (the future).

In the prayer of Moses (Psalm 90:12), the psalmist speaks about the brevity of life. One way we can treasure our lives is to realize that our days are numbered. We are born to die. With this in mind, the psalmist is telling us to use our time wisely. Each morning we wake up is an opportunity to take time to thank God for life and meditate on the Word of God.

Time is a precious resource given to each of us by the God who gave us life. It is not to be wasted, but used wisely in order to gain the maximum benefits of a treasured life. While there is a time for everything (Ecclesiastes 3:1), we cannot make or control it. We can only use the time we have been given by God. In Ephesians 5:15–17, the writer is suggesting to the believers at Ephesus that they should have a plan for living and so should we. We should pay attention to what we do each day and what occupies our time. Time spent in accordance with the word of God leads to a treasured life.

IN SEARCH OF A TREASURED LIFE

In James 4:14, the writer says: "Ye know not what shall be on tomorrow. For what is your life? It is even a vapor that appears for a little time and then vanishes away."

List three things that you should be doing now that you have put off for another time in your life.

(1) _____

(2) _____

(3) _____

If you kept a week-long journal (see the chapter on **Investment**), look at one day from your log and make a list of the things (like school, work, time with family and friends, watching TV, etc.) that occupy *most* of your time during the day. Make a separate list of what occupies the *least* of your time.

Three things that occupy *most of my time during the day*

(1) _____ _____

(2) _____

(3) _____

Three things that occupy the *least of my time during the day*

(1) _____

(2) _____

(3) _____

Are you satisfied with how you are using time?
Check one: ( ) Yes ( ) No

If yes, how can you make better use your time? I can make better use of my time by _____

Do you consult with God when making plans? Why or why not?

_____

_____

_____

_____

RELATED SCRIPTURES ABOUT TIME

(If you want to read more about what the Bible says about **time**, here are some related Scriptures. You may find others in your Bible reading. If you do, add them to the list.)

Job 14:1–14
Psalm 31:14–15; 39:5-6; 90:12
Proverbs 16:9
Ecclesiastes 3:1-8, 11
1 Thessalonians 5:1–3
Hebrews 3:12-15
James 4:13–15

COINS FOR YOUR TREASURE CHEST

(Entries in this section are additional quotes from other sources or thoughts written by the author. If you find more quotes on this topic, please add them along with the source of the quote.)

"Time will teach more than all our thoughts."
—Benjamin Disraeli

"You build a successful life a day at a time."
—Lou Holtz

"To love life is to love time. Time is the stuff life is made of."
—Benjamin Franklin

UNITY

"We are each other's harvest; we are each other's business;
we are each other's magnitude and bond."
—Gwendolyn Brooks

Y̶OUR LIFE IS TO BE TREASURED. A̶S MUCH AS IT DEPENDS ON YOU,
TRY TO LIVE IN **UNITY** *AND PEACE WITH OTHERS.*

 KEY SCRIPTURE

How good and pleasant it is when brothers live together in unity!
—Psalm 133:1 (NIV)

Unity is the state of being joined together as a whole. It is being in harmony or agreement with others. Unity is the quality or state of being one. The poet, John Donne said, *"No man is an island unto himself. We are all a part of the continent, all a part of the main."*

In Psalm 133, the psalmist suggests that it is good, pleasant and joyful when people live together in unity. It is the unity that comes down from above—from God. The point here is that unity in its truest sense can only come from God by the Holy Spirit. Rather than coming together to show solidarity with others for a special occasion or common cause, it is living daily in unity with others that leads one to a treasured life.

A common misconception about being in unity with others is that we must agree on everything. This is not the case. Unity does not require uniformity. What it does require is that we seek to be at peace with others, even when we disagree. There can be no peace without unity. One can disagree with another in a spirit of love and respect. We can respectfully agree to disagree. It does not appear that God intended that everyone should agree on things of minor importance.

In unity, there can be justice, love, mercy, and respect for everyone. We strengthen ourselves when we seek to strengthen others. Rather than dividing us, it is unity that binds us together.

IN SEARCH OF A TREASURED LIFE

Why do you think it is difficult to live in unity with those with whom we disagree?

_____

_____

_____

How do hatred, jealousy, backbiting, gossip, and envy contribute to problems with unity?

_____

_____

_____

The prayer that Jesus prays in John 17:20–23 is about unity. Jesus describes unity as being one with God, and others.

Take a few minutes to read and think about this prayer.

> *"I pray for these followers, but I am also praying for all those who believe in me because of their teaching. Father, I pray that they can be one. As you are in me and I am in you, I pray that they can also be one in us. Then the world will believe that you sent me. I have given these people the glory that you gave me so that they can be one, just as you and I are one. I will be in them and you will be in me so that they were completely one. Then the world will know that you sent me and that you loved them just as much as you loved me"* (NCV).

How important do you think being at one with God and others is to Jesus?

_____

_____

_____

_____

_____

RELATED SCRIPTURES ABOUT UNITY

(If you want to read more about what the Bible says about **unity**, here are some related Scriptures. You may find others in your Bible reading. If you do, add them to the list.)

Amos 3:3

Mark 9:50

John 17:23

Romans 6:5; 12:4–8, 16

1 Corinthians 1:10

Ephesians 1:10; 2:14; 4:3

Philippians 2:1–4

Colossians 3:13–14

1 Thessalonians 5:13

1 Peter 3:8

COINS FOR YOUR TREASURE CHEST

(Entries in this section are additional quotes from other sources or thoughts written by the author. If you find more quotes on this topic, please add them along with the source of the quote.)

"Men's hearts ought not to be set against one another, but set with one another, and all against evil only."
—Thomas Carlyle

"Whatever disunites man from God, also disunites man from man."
—Edmund Burke

"Unity is vision; it must have been part of the process of learning to see."
—Henry Adams

"It is not in numbers, but in unity that our great strength lies."
—Thomas Paine

VISION

"The only way you will be able to see life with clear vision
is when you view all of life from a Kingdom perspective."
—Tony Evans

Your life is to be treasured.
Have a **VISION** *for what you want to accomplish in your life.*

⚓ KEY SCRIPTURE

When people do not accept divine guidance, they run wild.
But whoever obeys the law is joyful.
—Proverbs 29:18 (NLT)

Vision is the act or power of imagination. It is seeing or conceiving of something before it becomes a reality. Vision is what connects our present life with our anticipated future. Although Proverbs 29:18 speaks about vision from a heavenly perspective, the important thread to be noted is that for a vision to be realized, some action is required. Joel Barker makes the necessity of vision with action clear when he says, *"Vision without action is merely a dream; action without vision just passes the time; vision with action can change the world."*

Attempting to go through life without a vision leads to a life of aimless wandering and hopelessness. A treasured life is not a hopeless life. It is life with meaning and purpose. It is a life grounded in the Word of God and full of possibilities for fulfillment and happiness. Vison gives us the capacity to see what is invisible to others and the audacity to make our dreams a reality.

Having a vision that connects with God's plan in creating us in the first place enables us to become all that God intends for us to be. We were born with the potential to live a meaningful and purposeful life to the fullest. True joy in our lives can come from having a vision that inspires us to daily pursue our goals.

🔍 IN SEARCH OF A TREASURED LIFE

What do you think Tony Evans mean by *"viewing all of life from a Kingdom perspective"*?

_____

_____

_____

In your wildest dreams, where do you imagine yourself 10 years in the future?

_____

Creating a Vision Statement

A **vision statement** is a clear statement of what you want to accomplish in life. It can set a clear path for focusing on where you want to be in your life with end goals in mind. Using the sample below as a guide, try to write a vision statement for your life in 25 words or less.

Sample Vision Statement:

My vision is to live a treasured life, balancing faith, family, and friends while using my God-given gifts for God's glory in serving others.

Your Vision Statement

_____

_____

_____

Now, using the sample below as a guide, try to edit down your statement to 15 words or less.

Sample Edited Vision Statement

I want to glorify God with a balanced, gifted, and treasured life that serves others.

Your Edited Vision Statement

_____

_____

_____

If you do not have a vision, please get someone who mentors you, or someone you respect and trust, to help you create your vision and write your statement.

RELATED SCRIPTURES ABOUT VISION

(If you want to read more about what the Bible says about **vision**, here are some related Scriptures. You may find others in your Bible reading. If you do, add them to the list.)

Psalm 37:4–5
Proverbs 3:5–6
Jeremiah 29:11
Amos 3:7
Habakkuk 2:3
John 15:7
Philippians 4:6–7
1 John 5:14–15

COINS FOR YOUR TREASURE CHEST

(Entries in this section are additional quotes from other sources or thoughts written by the author. If you find more quotes on this topic, please add them along with the source of the quote.)

"Where there is no vision, there is no hope."
—George Washington Carver

"If you are working on something exciting that you really care about, you don't have to be pushed. The vision pulls you."
—Steve Jobs

"It is a terrible thing to see and have no vision."
—Helen Keller

"By failing to have a vision, you are stripping yourself of every possible blessing, relationship, and opportunity."
—Steve Harvey

WISDOM

*"We are made wise not by the recollection of our past,
but by the responsibility for our future."*
—George Bernard Shaw

Your life is to be treasured. Have the
WISDOM *to seek guidance from the Word of God and
the assistance of others who can help you become a better you.*

 KEY SCRIPTURE

*If any of you lacks wisdom, you should ask God, who gives generously to all
without finding fault, and it will be given to you.*
—James 1:5 (NLT)

Wisdom is more than having mere knowledge. It is one's ability to apply the knowledge he or she possesses and the desire to make his or her life count. It is the ability to discern inner qualities and relationships. Wisdom is having insight. The guiding Scripture from the book of James informs us that wisdom is a gift from God available to anyone who asks in faith (James 1:5–8). Godly wisdom enables one to know God's plan for his or her life and live according to God's word.

King Solomon in the Bible was considered to be the wisest man who ever lived. When he became king of Israel, Solomon was asked by God in a dream to choose anything he desired. An "understanding heart" is what the king asked for and God gave it to him (1 King 3:9). Although he used the wisdom that God had given him to rule his kingdom, Solomon failed to apply that same wisdom to his personal life. We learn from Solomon that godly wisdom should be practiced in every aspect of our lives.

People who live a treasured life will *"Trust in the Lord with all their heart(s) and not depend on their own understanding. They will seek (God's) will in everything they do, counting on God to show them the right path to take"* (Proverbs 3:4–6). A Treasured life is one that is not impressed with or guided by personal wisdom, but guided by fear of the Lord while turning away from doing what is evil.

Q IN SEARCH OF A TREASURED LIFE

Someone has said, *"Be wise enough to walk away from the nonsense around you."* In what areas of your life are you making wise choices to walk away from the nonsense? Select one:

___ (a) at home
___ (b) at school
___ (c) in my neighborhood
___ (d) at work
___ (e) Other _____

In what areas of your life is it difficult, right now, for you to walk away from the nonsense around you? Select one:

___ (a) at home

___ (b) at school

___ (c) in my neighborhood

___ (d) at work

___ (e) Other _____

3. Talk with a family member, friend, mentor, or someone else you respect and trust to help you take the next step in search of a treasured life.

RELATED SCRIPTURES ABOUT WISDOM

(If you want to read more about what the Bible says about **widsom**, here are some related Scriptures. You may find others in your Bible reading. If you do, add them to the list.)

Exodus 31:3
Deuteronomy 4:6
Psalm 16:7; 32:8; 51:6
Proverbs 2:5–7; 3:13; 4:5–10; 5:1–6; 10:31; 28:5
Ecclesiastes 2:26; 7:12–19
Isaiah 2:3; 43:6
2 Corinthians 4:6
1 John 5:20

COINS FOR YOUR TREASURE CHEST

(Entries in this section are additional quotes from other sources or thoughts written by the author. If you find more quotes on this topic, please add them along with the source of the quote.)

"The art of being wise is the art of knowing what to overlook."
—William James

"Life is full of perils, but the wise man ignores those that are inevitable."
—Bertrand Arthur William Russell

"Knowledge comes from learning, wisdom comes from living."
—Anthony Douglas Williams

"Knowing yourself is the beginning of all wisdom."
—Aristotle

Six Ethics of Life
Before you pray—Believe
Before you speak—Listen
Before you spend—Earn
Before you write—Think
Before you quit—Try
Before you die—Live!
—Author Unknown

EXPECTATIONS

"High achievement always takes place in the framework of high expectations"
—Charles Kettering

YOUR LIFE IS TO BE TREASURED.
HAVE HIGH **EXPECTATIONS** *FOR WHAT YOU WANT TO ACHIEVE*
WHILE LIVING A LIFE THAT GLORIFIES GOD AND LEAVES A GOOD
EXAMPLE FOR OTHERS TO FOLLOW.

 KEY SCRIPTURE

For I know the plans I have for you, says the Lord. They are plans for good and not disaster, to give you a future and a hope.
—Jeremiah 29:11 (NLT)

Expectations are our inner desires or intent to "be" or "do." Expectations are intentions to achieve rather than reactions to something that has already happened. To have expectations is having something to look forward to rather than resorting to *"would haves," "should haves," "could haves"* after the fact.

People who have expectations of treasuring the life that God has blessed them with already know that God has a plan for their life. *"They aspire to be their best selves rather than live a life of mediocrity. They expect to take what is good and desire to be great. The ability to do this requires learning to say 'no' to the good, so that they can say 'yes' to the best"* (John Maxwell).

The point made in Proverbs 23:7 is that we are defined by what we think in our hearts. Our actions are guided by our internal thoughts. In our heart is where the seed of expectation resides. Someone said that we will always tend to fulfill our own expectations of ourselves. In order to perform as a winner, we must see ourselves as a winner (Zig Ziglar). With God in our hearts and our lives we can expect to have joy, peace, and contentment. We can be all that God planned for our lives even before we were born.

IN SEARCH OF A TREASURED LIFE

What are 10 expectations that you have for your life?

1. _____

2. _____

3. _____

4. _____

5. _____

6. _____

7. _____

8. _____

9. _____

10. _____

List the three most important expectations:

1. _____

2. _____

3. _____

Which of your top three expectations match most with God's plan for your life, as you understand it from Scripture? Why?

_____

_____

_____

RELATED SCRIPTURES ABOUT EXPECTATIONS

(If you want to read more about what the Bible says about **expectations**, here are some related Scriptures. You may find others in your Bible reading. If you do, add them to the list.)

Psalm 62:5

Proverbs 24:14

Jeremiah 33:3

John 1:12

2 Corinthians 9:8

Philippians 1:20; 4:6

Hebrews 11:1

COINS FOR YOUR TREASURE CHEST

(Entries in this section are additional quotes from other sources or thoughts written by the author. If you find more quotes on this topic, please add them along with the source of the quote.)

"Life is largely a matter of expectations."
—Horace

"Nobody rises to low expectations."
—Calvin Lloyd

"I have been bent and broken, but—I hope—into a better shape.
—Charles Dickens, *Great Expectations*

"Be determined to make the rest of your life, the best of your life."
—Unknown

YOUTHFULNESS

"Good habits formed at youth make all the difference."
—Aristotle

YOUR LIFE IS TO BE TREASURED. EMBRACE YOUR
YOUTHFULNESS *BY THINKING AND ACTING YOUR AGE*
WHILE REMEMBERING GOD WHO GAVE YOU THE GIFT OF LIFE.

 **KEY SCRIPTURE**

Don't let the excitement of youth cause you to forget your creator.
Honor him in your youth before you grow old and say,
Life is not pleasant anymore.
—Ecclesiastes 12:1 (NLT)

Youthfulness is the state of being young, energetic, growing, developing, and having vitality. If you are a young person, you are one of our future leaders. Embrace your youthfulness with the awareness that God wants to use you at all stages of your life. The Bible records many accounts of youth who despite their age were used by God for his glory. When you develop a relationship with God while you are young, God will guide you throughout your life.

The Bible tells children to obey their parents because it is both the right thing to do, and it is what God expects. A treasured life that embraces youthfulness is one where one obeys and honors parents and elders while honoring, loving, and following God with one's heart, mind, and soul. As we grow older, we maintain our youthfulness by taking care of our bodies, nourishing our minds, remaining young at heart, and living a treasured life.

IN SEARCH OF A TREASURED LIFE

If you are still living with your parents, on a scale of 1 to 10, with 10 being the highest, how obedient are you to your parents? _____

If you are a young adult living away from home, on a scale of 1 to 10, with 10 being the highest, how obedient are you to your parents? _____

If you have a family of your own and no longer have your parents to guide you, how obedient are you to God? (Select one)
____ (a) very obedient
____ (b) to some extent; I slip sometimes
____ (c) The thought of being obedient to God never really crossed my mind
____ (d) I'm working on this
____ (e) Other _____.

As a young person, I can honor God by (select one)
____ (a) obeying my parents
____ (b) going to church
____ (c) staying out of trouble
____ (d) thanking God for life
____ (e) Other _____.

I can honor my parents by (select one)

___ (a) obeying my parents

___ (b) doing well in school

___ (c) doing my chores without complaining

___ (d) being respectful to others

___ (e) Other _____ _____

RELATED SCRIPTURES ABOUT YOUTHFULNESS

(If you want to read more about what the Bible says about **youthfulness**, here are some related Scriptures. You may find others in your Bible reading. If you do, add them to the list.)

Genesis 37:2; 39:1–4

Ruth 1:16–18

Psalm 71:5

Proverbs 22:6

Ecclesiastes 3:1–8; 11:9

Jeremiah 1:7–9

Lamentations 3:27

Ezekiel 16:20

1 Timothy 4:12

2 Timothy 2:22

COINS FOR YOUR TREASURE CHEST

(Entries in this section are additional quotes from other sources or thoughts written by the author. If you find more quotes on this topic, please add them along with the source of the quote.)

"Youth is to all the glad season of life, but often only by what it hopes, not by what it attains or escapes."
—Thomas Carlyle

"Youth lives on hope, old age on memories."
—Unknown

"You are young only once, and if you work it right, once is enough."
—Joe E. Lewis

"Youth is happy because it has the ability to see beauty. Anyone who keeps the ability to see beauty never grows old."
—Franz Kafka

ZEAL

"Do all the good you can, in all the ways you can,
to all the souls you can, in every place you can,
at all the times you can, with all the zeal you can
as long as you can."
—John Wesley

---

*YOUR LIFE IS TO BE TREASURED. LIVE YOUR LIFE WITH **ZEAL**—*
A SENSE OF ENTHUSIASM AND PASSION IN SEARCH OF YOUR PURPOSE FOR LIVING.

 KEY SCRIPTURE

Never be lazy, but work hard and serve the Lord enthusiastically.
—Romans 12:11 (NLT)

Zeal is having a passion for something. It is great energy or enthusiasm that a person devotes to a worthwhile cause or goal. Ralph Waldo Emerson said, *"Nothing great was ever achieved without enthusiasm."* With zeal, a person has an inner drive or determination to be successful in life.

In a religious sense, zeal means devotion to God or some religious cause. If you have a zeal for life, you will have a passion for living a fruitful and productive life that both honors God and serves others. To this point, it is good to follow the advice of Confucius who once said, "When you are laboring for others, let it be with the same zeal as if it were for yourself." This would be difficult, if not impossible, to do without loving God and your neighbor as you love yourself.

IN SEARCH OF A TREASURED LIFE

List three things that you have a passion for doing at this point in your life.

1. _____

2. _____

3. _____

Briefly explain how each thing that you listed would contribute to a productive life that glorifies God and serves others?

_____

_____

_____

_____

_____

RELATED SCRIPTURES ABOUT ZEAL

(If you want to read more about what the Bible says about **zeal**, here are some related Scriptures. You may find others in your Bible reading. If you do, add them to the list.)

Isaiah 59:17

1 Corinthians 9:27

2 Corinthians 3:12; 8:7

Galatians 6:9

Philippians 1:27; 2:16

2 Thessalonians 3:13

2 Timothy 2:10

1 Peter 2:2

2 Peter 1:10

Revelation 3:19

COINS FOR YOUR TREASURE CHEST

(Entries in this section are additional quotes from other sources or thoughts written by the author. If you find more quotes on this topic, please add them along with the source of the quote.)

"Zeal will do more than knowledge."
—William Hazlitt

"Zeal is a volcano on the peak of which the grass of indecisiveness does not grow."
—Khalil Gibran

"Success is due less to ability than to zeal."
—Charles Buxton

"Catch on fire with enthusiasm and people will come for miles to watch you burn."
—Unknown

END NOTES

Acceptance

1. Quote taken from *The Centering Moment* by Howard Thurman, copyright 1969 by Harper & Row, New York, NY; p. 15.
2. Quote taken from *My Utmost for His Highest* by Oswald Chambers, edited by James Reimann, copyright 1992 by Oswald Chambers Publications Association, Ltd. Used by permission of Discovery House Publishers, Grand Rapids, MI 49501. All rights reserved.
3. Coin quote written by the author.

Balance

1. Quote taken from *Concerning the Inner Life* by Evelyn Underhill, copyright 1926 by E. P. Dutton & Company, Inc., New York; p. 84.
2. Quote from www.brainyquote.com/quotes/authors/rumi.
3. Coin quote written by the author.

Contentment

1. Quote from www.brainyquote.com/quotes/j/josephaddison.
2. Quote from Carl Dreizler and Mary E. Ehemann, "52 Ways to Lose Weight" in *Lists to Live By For Everything that Really Matters*, compiled by Alice Gray, Steve Stephens, John Van Diest, copyright 1999, published by Multnomah Publishers, p. 201. All rights reserved.

Discipline

1. Quote from www.forbes.com/quotes/author/arthur-s-adams.
2. Quote from *Pearls of Power for Possibility Thinkers* by Robert H. Schuller, p. 105, copyright 1997 by Robert Harold Schuller, published by Countryman, a division of Thomas Nelson, Inc., Nashville, Tennessee. All rights reserved.

Endurance

1. Quote from www.inspirationalstories.com/quotes/henry-wadsworth-longfellow.
2. Quote from *Webster's Book of Quotations*, copyright 1994 by PMC Publishing Company, Inc. New York, NY, p. 84.
3. Quote from www.goodreads.com/author/quotes/769264-Vivian_Greene.

Faith, Family, and Friends

1. Quote from *Webster's Book of Quotations*, p. 95.
2. Quote from H. Jackson Brown Jr., *A Hero in Every Heart*, p. 20, copyright 1996 by H. Jackson Brown, Jr. and Robert Spizman, published by Thomas Nelson, Inc., Nashville, Tennessee. All rights reserved.
3. Quote taken from "To Be A Good Friend" in *Lists to Live By For Everything that Really Matters*, by Alice Gray, Steve Stephens, John Van Diest, copyright 1999 by Multnomah Publishers, Inc., p. 50.
4. Quote from *Webster's Book of Quotations*, p. 106.
5. Coin quote on Family written by the author.

Glorify God

1. Quote from *My Utmost for His Highest* by Oswald Chambers (11/16), edited by James Reimann, copyright 1992 by Oswald Chambers Publications Assn., Ltd., and used by permission of Discovery House Publishers, Grand Rapids, MI 49501. All rights reserved.
2. Quote from www.glorifygod/lifeandtruth;pinterset/SayingsandGod. in.pinterset.com.

Humility

1. Quote on "Humility" by Confucius taken from *Webster's' Book of Quotations*, p. 122.

Investment

1. Quote on "Investment" taken from section on "Friendship" by Howard Ward Beecher from *Webster's Book of Quotations*, p. 108.

2. Quote taken from reading on 3/16, p. 84, *My Daily Psalms and Prayers* by Christine A. Dallman and Randy Petersen, copyright 2010, 2012 by Publications International, Ltd. All rights reserved.
3. Quote by George Bernard Shaw taken from p. 60, *Inspirational Meditations: a collection of inspirational thoughts and images*, copyright 2011 by Parragon Books Ltd. All rights reserved.
4. Quote by John Ruskin taken from *Inspirational Meditations*, p. 91.

Joyfulness

1. Quote by Dale Carnegie taken from https://www.brainyquote.com/quotes/quotes/d/dalecarneg106496.html
2. Author Unknown, "Recipe for Happiness" taken from wall plaque in department store.
3. Quote by Robert Schuller taken from *Pearls of Power for Possibility Thinkers*, p. 16.
4. Quote by Z. Gordon B. Hinckley taken from www.goodreads.com/quotes/66093
5. Quote on "Joy" taken from the writings of Dr. Norman Vincent Peale in *Guideposts* Outreach Publication on "Joy", p. 5, copyright 2014 by Guideposts.

Kindness

1. Quote on "Kindness" by William Penn taken from *Webster's Book of Quotations*, p. 139.
2. Quote on "Kindness" by Sara Fielding taken from *Inspirational Meditations*, p. 72.
3. Quote on "Kindness" by Albert Schweitzer taken from www.quotation-sp.com/quote/2391.html.

Love

1. Quote on "Love" by Henry Ward Beecher taken from https://www.brainyquote.com/quotes/quotes/h/henrywardb150046.html.
2. Anonymous quote on "Love" taken from wall plaque in department store.

3. Quote on "Love" taken from *What Keeps Me Standing*, copyright 2003 by Dennis Kimbro, published by Doubleday, a division of Random House, Inc., p. 145.

Moderation

1. Quote on "Moderation" by Seneca taken from *Webster's Book of Quotations*, p. 161

2. Quote from Cicero taken from *Webster's Book of Quotations*, p. 161.

Name

1. Quote about "Name" taken from *What Makes You So Strong: Sermons of Joy and Strength from Jeremiah A. Wright*; edited by Jini Kilgore Ross; copyright 1993 by Judson Press, Valley Forge, Pa, p. 133. All rights reserved.

2. Quote about "Name" by Thomas Fuller taken from *Webster's Book of Quotations*, p. 165

Opportunity

1. Quote about "Opportunity" by Samuel Johnson taken from *Webster's Book of Quotations*, p. 172.

2. Quote about "Opportunity" taken from *Touchpoints Bible Promises: God's Answers for your Daily Needs*; copyright 2000 by V. Gilbert Beers and Ronald A. Beers; Tyndale House publishers, Inc., p. 170. All rights reserved.

3. Quote about "Opportunity" taken from goodlifequotation.com.

4. Quote about "Opportunity" taken from picturequotes.com.

Purpose

1. Quote about "Purpose" taken from Sayings about Life and Purpose on Pinterest.com.

2. Quote about "Purpose" taken from Rick Warren.

3. Quote on "Prayer" by Alexis Carrell taken from *Webster's Book of Quotations*, p. 182.

4. Quote on "Purpose" taken from Albert Schweitzer.

5. Quote on "Patience" by Francis De Sales taken from www.very-bestquotes.com.
6. Chinese proverb quotation on "Patience" taken from *Webster's Book of Quotations*, p. 175.

Quietness
1. Quote on "Quietness" by Euripides taken from *Webster's Book of Quotations*, p. 190.
2. Quote on "spending quiet time with God" taken from *Our Daily Bread*, August 17, 2013.
3. Quote on "having a quiet mind" by Hamilton Wright Mabie taken from *Webster's Book of Quotations*, p. 190.
4. Quote by Friedrich Nietzsche taken from livinglifefully.com.
5. Quote on "quiet the mind" by Ma Jaya Sati Bhagavali taken from Oky-Day.com

Respect
1. Quote on "Respect" taken from wall poster; author unknown.
2. Quote on "Respect" taken from wall poster, author unknown.
3. Quote on "Respect" by Mildred Taylor taken from tradingphrases.com.
4. Quote on "Respect" by Mahatma Gandhi taken from www.StatusMind.com.
5. Quote on "Respect" by the author.

Standards
1. Quote on "Standards" by Roy E. Disney taken from pinterest.com.
2. Quote on "Standards" by Dalai Lama taken from https//www.dailyinspirationalquotesin/2013/01/theultimate.
3. Quote on "Standards" by Mahatma Gandhi taken from www.notable-quotes.com/g/gandhi_mahatma.html.

Time
1. Quote on "Time" by Hans Christian Anderson taken from *Webster's Book of Quotations*, p. 218.
2. Quote on "Time by Benjamin Disraeli taken from *Webster's Book of Quotations*, p. 219.

3. Quote on "Time" by Lou Holtz taken from www.azquotes.com/Authors>L>Lou Holtz.

4. Quote on "Time" by Benjamin Franklin taken from *Franklin Guidebook*; copyright 1989 by Franklin International Institute, Inc. All rights reserved.

Unity

1. Quote on "Unity" by Gwendolyn Brooks taken from www.azquotes.com/Authors>G> Gwendolyn Brooks.

2. Quote on "Unity" by Thomas Carlyle taken from *Webster's Book of Quotations*, p. 227.

3. Quote on "Unity" by Edmund Burke taken from www.azquotes.com/Authors>E> Edmund Burke.

4. Quote on "Unity" by Henry Adams taken from www.azquotes.com>Authors>H> Henry Adams.

5. Quote on "Unity" by Thomas Paine taken from www.azquotes.com>Authors>T> Thomas Paine.

Vision

1. Quote on "Vision" by Tony Evans taken from www.TheKingdomAgendaBook.com.

2. Quote on "Vision" by George Washington Carver taken from www.brainyquote.com/quotes/keywords/Vision.html.

3. Quote on "Vision" by Steve Jobs taken from www.azquotes.com>Authors>S> Steve Jobs.

4. Quote on "Vision" by Helen Keller taken from www.azquotes.com>Authors>H> Helen Keller.

5. Quote on "Vision" by Steve Harvey taken from *Act Like a Success, Think Like a Success*; www.pinterest.com/dw2d/steve-harvey- quotes.

Wisdom

1. Quote on "Wisdom" by George Bernard Shaw taken from www.brainyquote.com/quotes/topics/topic_Wisdom.

2. Quote on "Wisdom" by William James taken from *Webster's Book of Quotations*, p. 237.

3. Quote on "Wisdom" by Bertrand Arthur William Russell taken from *Webster's Book of Quotations*, p. 237.
4. Quote on "Wisdom" by Anthony Douglas Williams taken from http://goodreads.com/quotes/7670248-knowledge-comes-from.
5. Quote on "Wisdom" by Aristotle taken from *Inspirational Meditations*, p. 59, copyright 2011 by Parragon Books Ltd. All rights reserved.
6. "Six Ethics of Life," taken from wall poster art found in Ross Department Store; author unknown.

Expectations

1. Quote on "Expectations" by Charles Kettering taken from www.brainyquote.com/quotes/keywords/expectations.html.
2. Quote on "Expectations" by Horace taken from www.brainyquote.com/quotes/quotes/h/horace152468.html.
3. Quote on "Expectations" by Calvin Lloyd taken from www.brainyquote.com/quotes/keywords/expectations.html.
4. Quote on "Expectations" by Charles Dickens from *Great Expectations* taken from www.azquotes.com.Authors.c.Charles Dickens.
5. Quote, "Be determined to make the rest of your life, the best of your life" taken from wall plaque in a novelty store in Martha's Vineyard; author unknown.

Youthfulness

1. Quote on "Youthfulness" by Aristotle taken from www.brainyquote.com/quotes/keywords/youth.html.
2. Quote on "Youthfulness" by Thomas Carlyle taken from *Webster's Book of Quotations*, p. 243.
3. Quote, on "Youthfulness" by an unknown author taken from www.brainyquote.com/quotes/keywords/youth.html.
4. Quote on "Youthfulness" by Joe E. Lewis taken from www.brainyquote.com/quotes/quotes/joeelewis151195.html.
5. Quote on "Youthfulness" by Franz Kafka taken from www.brainyquote.com/quotes/keywords/youth.html.

Zeal

1. Quote on "Zeal" by John Wesley taken from *Congratulations on Your Achievement* compiled by Kathy Shutt, published by Barbour Publishing, Inc. All rights reserved.

2   Quote on "Zeal" by William Hazlitt taken from www.goodreads.com/quotes/tag/zeal.

3. Quote on "Zeal" by Khalil Gibran taken from www.goodreads.com/quotes/tag/zeal.

4. Quote on "Zeal" by Charles Buxton taken from www.goodreads.com/quotes/tag/zeal.

5. Quote on "Zeal" by unknown author taken from www.goodreads.com/quotes/tag/zeal.